ABSENCES

A SEQUENCE

JOHN A. GRIFFIN

 The Esthetic Apostle

PARTS I - VII

Caoineadh

You have suffered through the fluted bones
of the white shells and the horns of hunger,
you have survived the winter's ash
and the snows blasting the stones to lead,
you have warmed the blood of the anaemic year
and found in the refuse heaps of hope
the accoutrements to cope, the thaw of warm words
and melting sighs on frozen windowpanes,
the blades of ice and the unfrosted tears of the dew.
Here is a grey, pedestrian morn and a well
that flushes out the past of all that is past,
avalanching cones from the withered woods,
the minnows dead and the streams all dead,
and consciousness of itself flowing into drains —
You have arisen with the cries from apocalyptic skies,
and walked along the strands where the sands recede
to where the dust of the ages gathers and flows,
and what ebbs withdraws what mercy sows
in the caged heart, peace and joy and love
and the sad remembrance of remembered things.

Relic

It is November and a concussed fog hangs above the lake,
it was bullied and harried there from the purple trees –
Dusk smokes the icy air, inhales an ashen mist and exhales
a blue luminescent light that shimmers in the cloudless sky
and then is gone. Behind the hills are rocks and ruins,
castles and dead groves, sumps and reeds and mossy drains.
The leaden roofs were melted into bullets, and the bronze bells
and brass escutcheons were beaten into blades.
Those hills were shrill once with the cries of the hunted,
but now they've grown silent as an aftermath of blood,
that knows only the cost of an illegitimate patrimony.
These days we gather along the shore and launch our rafts
into tranquil tides, or we row out into the balmy morning mist
and skirt the woods, whose firs are furred with frost.
You can hear the swoosh and the slap of powdery pillows
falling onto eiderdowns of snow and you can hear
the frozen meadows crack and groan and thaw,
birds forage here and break their beaks on the solid earth,
but already the grubs have wormed their way back
through cuffs and cages of bone to this sunken river bank.

Icarus Complex

You have been falling out of life all your life,
parachuted out of the darkness
and plunged through soundless space,
the seas beneath you are full of blood and tears,
and the earth's a graveyard of ploughed-up bones.
Bats tap and drain your veins as you fall along,
and hawks snap the lines that keep you airborne.
Missiles are shot from the deepest depths
and their barbs and blades tear you asunder.
What vessel dropped you into freefall,
and what forces still drag you on
or postpone the inevitable descent to doom?
Do you know where these winds will take you
and for how long more? Do you try to steer a course?
Your flesh is worn and hangs on splintered bones,
your eyes can only see the end of seeing
as they tumble through blind corridors of remorse.
You've been falling out of life all your life,
and now only know this euphoria without epiphany,
this featherless, wingless flight without end.

Aurora

A mist rolls the dusk over into night and banks it
where charged vapours gather and borealis glows,
waves of chilled fog strop the winter air
and knead and numb our rash temples raw –
What cuts the light from itself, aura by sight,
also ices the chthonic corridors of our brain,
grips our frozen hearts into fists of quartz
then thaws then melts them back to tears again.
We've sailed the Arctic seas of our tears to where
they harden into desolation's bergs – North winds
drone through luminescent organs of ice,
gothic walls quake and crack, towers topple
and a white city thaws into the electric ocean.
We find refuge in a ghetto of frozen caves
and realize whatever magnetizes polarizes:
We're spun out of control too and unreeled here,
fed on the frosted, brittle lines that tie us to the deeps.
Day breaks and we're woven back into our element,
condensed and then vaporized and now snowed anew
over the grey fields where our names are buried.

Mad Medusa's Lament

The trees in the garden outside your window whisper
of the grave and their secrets fall as the leaves fall,
smothering your plot with subterfuge and decay.
The Autumn finds you alone with your grief.
You will endure it till the final fall of the withered leaves
plays its Death Fugue in the echo-chambers of your heart.
You can hear your funeral faintly passing above,
like tears of dew melting on graveside grass—
premonitions gather there and presage a grief
as palpable as any canker or fever in the blood.
This is your anachronism, misplaced and displaced,
like the exile searching for the proper word or gesture
to put to right what spite had swept away,
the fabric the years had woven into love,
now torn and ripped to shreds. Nothing remains
but the peripatetic valedictions of your homesick heart.
But should they not have named the hollow wind after you,
and the sunlight too, that you propitiate the skies
with your abject cries? Fate and Fury force you
into the shadows where a manic malice descends.

The Subtract

There are hedgehogs in the scented rows
and sparrows in the green brackets,
slugs square the mint leaves and worms coil
into roots to multiply before they die:
The curtains of logic close on rusty rails,
and mites farm the demon dust with dew.
There's a stain so shadowed with itself
it's not abstruse enough to stay gone forever,
and the bloated, drunken fleas cannot fathom
the unctuous tares of our blood. A sundial
wears a smile of shadow now the winter is done.
Is this not the sky you wanted, the sun you sought,
evenings doting and senile, gardens teeming,
and the old incantations tolling and teasing out
new subtracts from the same fixed formulae —
Here is the calculus of memory and forgetting,
loving and begetting — shells and moulted skins
strewn like the scraps of time, poppies weighted
with rain, the bees absent, and the pollen amuck
amidst the balms of musk and murder and manky ruin.

Monk's Elm

Do you recall the spaces opened by the sun in the shadows
of youth, infancy's tongue tongue-tied by waves of wrath,
the muslin curtains, the dust and the chimes and sometimes cries
from the darkness at the centre of a scene, a cut-out scene,
punched through a hole in memory and shaped to fit everywhere
except where it most belonged in your heart of hours?
Do you recall the black puddle in your path you could not cross?
Your whole world became unreal and suspended at its core,
without co-ordinates, you bore in your arms your naked, infant life,
you took up residence in absence there and dipped your hands
in the blood of light to finger-paint your past anew:
This was the room you knew, your room, smelling of sour milk
and fat, with shadows off their heads and the empty spaces
whispering of dead kings, cruelty's wings, and voyages out
steered by silence into the unsaid tides —presumption's jetty
ran to embrace you into sanctum's shore, but awake at last
among the hills and the spring fields, with not a current in sight,
but a sea's rhythm in your veins and an Ophelia invocation rippling
on every stream, you finally waded out to where your centre rose
and there you sank and drowned in the inky well of yourself.

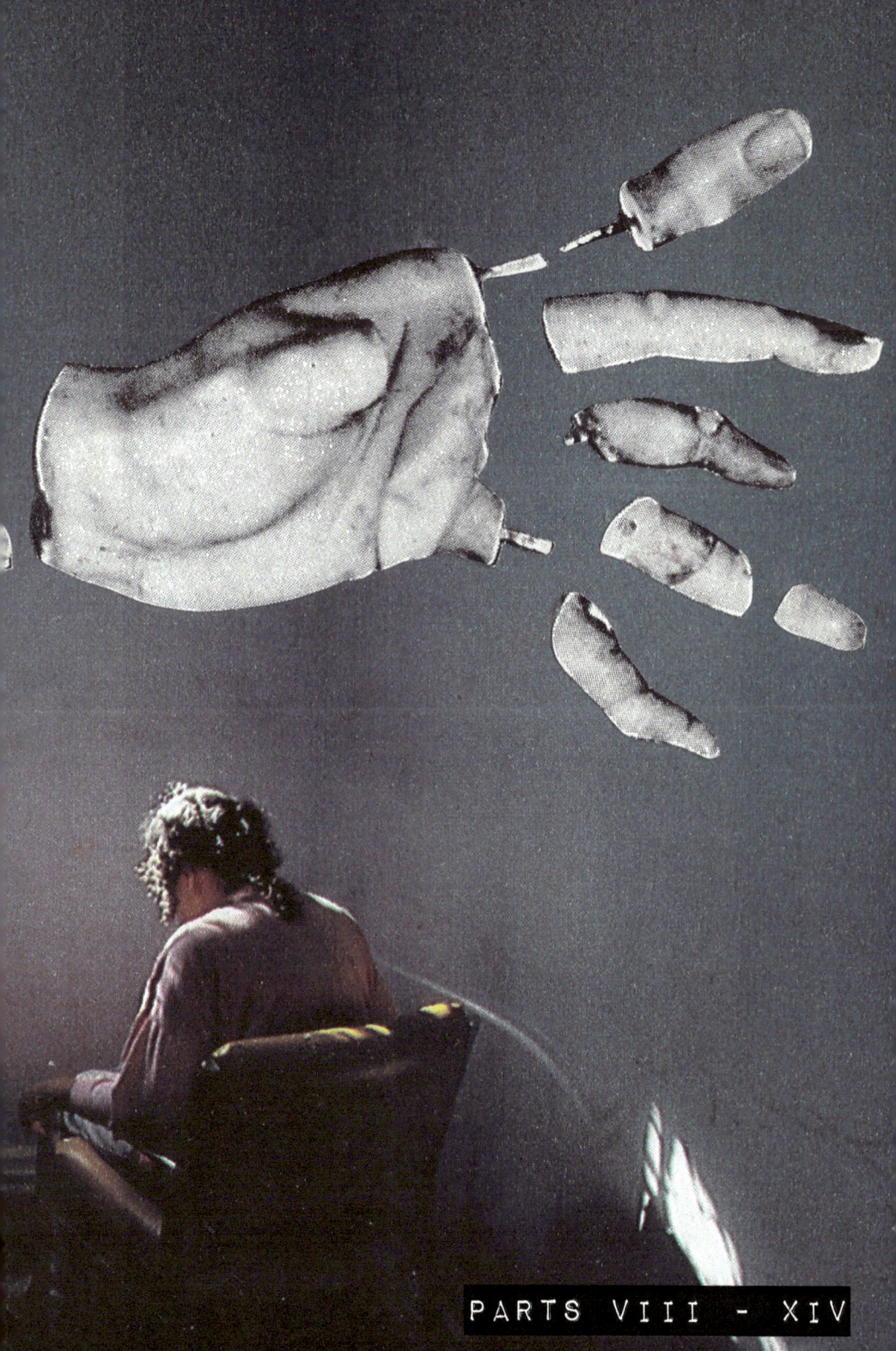

PARTS VIII - XIV

Asylum

When the moon rained down its dust and stones,
I was lost in the desert of supplication, I crawled
through the sand-fogged air and searched everywhere –
The north wind circled and then the rains came,
I heard the Sphinx's cry and I too cried out
for the air that breathes hope back into despair.
The islands of the moon are in my heart
and a cosmic sea inks my veins, I bleed darkness,
but I know there's a golden thread spun by the sun
that I can belay back to perfumed greenery:
Over the next dune and past the craters of the moon
is my love-oasis – no white noise resounds there,
only silence avalanching from the mute mountains
where the climbers of my dreams clamber and drop
into that dawn that is never born. When I look up,
I can see myself from afar, as if in a dream,
abseiling away through the dark pulse and pull
of every rise and fall – the moon is full in me
the way the air inhabits air, and I can feel its tug
like waves breaking on the shores of consciousness.

Leaf Storm

A child died the moment another child was born –
Two screams, one for grief and one for labour's end.
In the blighted groves, parasitic eggs swelled entropic,
rot gathered, and leaves fell through the dying season.
Until something moves time is eternal ...
Here, even the light falls like birds alighting.
Luminous greys threaten rain, but rain does not come,
only the ghosts of jasmine and the aromas of death,
camphor smells in the recesses of recall,
and the premonitory cries of the curlews.
A diabolical wind eclipses and quarantines the sun,
and all the almond trees, where the wretched built
their homes of ash are smothered in the dusty dark,
lizards appear on the floors of death chambers,
and the calloused hands that cultivated rosemary
and nard bleed and then stop forever,
a woman begs for lemon balm, her yellow eyes
open and hex, and a tangle of thorns tightens.
Everywhere the phantom harvest is ended and ruin
stares from the bare ceiba trees in the graveyard.

Perseus' Complaint

How can a ship be towed along by a mountain?
Yet here is the black lodestone of your life,
tugging your barge of years down rivers of time.
Is that you piloting grief under a funeral flag,
with a white flag stowed for surrender?
Is that a rock of light in your dark estuary?
Are you the vessel, the pilgrim, or the cargo?
Or some Pythagorean phantom cranking
the wheel till decrepitude steers you ashore?
What's gone cannot be retrieved even though
echoes still resound and dejection's daydreams
are transfused with blood – something else insists
on walking abroad and pounding grief's pavement,
a sound in search of an absent space to sound,
or waters winnowing waste in death pools,
where minnows swim in ever-decreasing circles
towards that vanishing point into absence:
The end winds commodiously back to the beginning,
and circles swirl ever inwards towards that focal point,
where the flesh migrates back into thought.

Axolotl
~After Julio Cortazar~

You entered the golden bead of the Axolotl's dead eye,
and what you saw distorted in that unfathomable depth,
diaphanous yet inscrutable, stony but alluring, and primal,
was your own mystery staring out at you: whatever wrought
that thought-creature, neither fish nor lizard, metamorphosed
you in its cannibalism of gold amid the sculpted greys and greens
of the aquarium, and left you gazing with expressionless calm.
The city fanned its peacock tail now the winter's lent
was spent and the spring sighed awake through gills of mist.
You could smell the fog in the humid spaces between your fear,
and you could hear the hopeless meditation of the silent shell
and the mute testimony, where larval limbs morphed and moved,
you could feel the implacable stare of the immobile amphibian,
whose lidless eyes can see past the dark, your dark,
and through the night with its lurid shapes and horrors,
its holed webs and honeycombs, its weeds and eels,
its seas of stars, and its endless migrations flowing back
to that état second, where all dimensions start,
and the impassive stones of its cold eyes glow gold
then rosy-red then fish-scale silver then blank to black.

In Der Strafkolonie

I opened the Black Book of the night because a chill
had crawled along my skin. It was the braille
of absence tracing its sentence on my flesh,
inscribing its embossed diktat across my loss.
I wear the scars on the book of my skin like sin.
In the Penal Colony, the past is a stylus dipped in blood,
its nib fits into glyphs and ruts and it cuts furrows
so deep in you even the light bleeds through –
Its harrow needle quivers above your exposed heart
and darns what you cannot read but only feel,
the insular but accursed art, grief's calligraphy,
whose script is stitched and sown into the gutters
of your Doomsday Book. Oaths cannot reprieve
the damned like you, for what is calibrated and written
has chosen you for its theme and for its prayer,
and cannot be swayed by love's codex or assuaged
by mercy's cries. Even thought is martyred and transfigured,
and yet at the midway hour, the rapture point of your pain,
your body begins to apprehend through its delirium
that wounds are words in the night's Black Book.

Magus Im Norden

Outside the city walls, where chestnuts fall
and snowflakes strobe and fleck the dark,
a man rides on a white horse across black ice —
he has the Tundra in his eyes and the kabbalah
beating in his heart, and what he leaves behind
leads nowhere beautifully, like God's footprints:
track his traces if you can and cross like him
the wastes until you too reach your Golgotha.
Now wait there, but do not expect an angel
to wring from your ragged and sunken veins
the rhapsody of the risen blood, nor that anguish
will renew redemption's pulse, and do not expect
reason to anoint your closed lids with light,
for we must shut our eyes to see the way to heaven:
clench your palms of peace into fists of belief
and pound at pardon's door. The Magus of the North
lies within, for he has reached his journey's end,
and now he's flung across his funeral bed,
though death is not yet born and the broken rib
has not yet paid its debt to sin or disbelief.

Beyond the Plateau

How could you eclipse and then repeal our sun?
Did we not share the same shadow beneath it?
And when we walked abroad did not the same air
close round our melded going? Our fused flesh
was so indistinguishable in its binder space
that not even fission could have sundered it,
but now that vessel is tenanted only by absence,
the air is divided from itself and cannot house
a single echo: silence shapes us for its mnemonic,
but has plunged us so deep in the dismal dark
even forgetfulness has forgot what we were –
Curiosity, memory's orphan, got lost inside our loss
and cannot find out why, it ghosts our parting
and comes only to sneer as though desertion
were a bedlamite and despair its muted mouth?
This was not the life we wanted, it was not for this
we dreamed each other's dreams or built our nest
on air, or hung our garden there with forget-me-nots.
Nothing turned out as planned, even the turning out
was dammed with broken shells, and rot, and blue ruin.

Black Widow

It seems the widow's webs are once more
spun across his days — what glistens lures —
so, mesmerized he staggers into seams and snares.
He raises a shield of ardor to ward off
tacky threads, but it quivers in the air
and sets her strings pulsating. Her tuned harp
plays at its proper pitch and waves undulate
as though a fold in air shimmered with a beat
that was his own arrhythmic heartbeat.
He sways and tumbles, he heaves and falls —
her fibres dance and ripple — he squirms —
her nerves and sinews twitch and quaver,
she plays him into intervals of slowed air —
he jounces with the shivers — she agitates
her rigging, hypnotic cords whip the space
between them, delicately her derricks twist,
her cables turn, she loosens the eyes of knots
and reels him into her deadly noose
where the tackle drops — he drops, doped legs
genuflect and splay across his only get-away.

Graiai

When they shared the eye, tears were also passed between,
not that the next socket ever needed teary lubrication,
but if there was a nut to crack or a jerky to chew on,
a plaque-stained mandible was always preferable –
All those parts going back and forth symbiotically
with a repugnant synergy bound their bodies as one,
and soon enough they were thinking as one as well,
not that these crones ever needed to explain their antics.
They believed they were driven by some innate necessity,
which only a special concord like theirs could enjoin.
But try playing along or asking for the loan of an organ
and they'd promptly go ape-shit and start swapping round
that one good eye just to glare at you in anger and disgust.
Who knows how the habit began or why it first took hold.
They protected it like it was some secret incestuous shame
only they could disclose, except they would not disclose it –
They had even devised ways of burying it in the rituals
of their dishing out, but Perseus knew there was more to it
than met the eye and when he stole theirs to kill Medusa,
he saw Right through the blind logic of an eye for an eye.

Portents

In the lull after late bells a leaf falls
and a blade of grass cuts a tear in two,
a gate swings on a hinge of absence
between the meadow and the wind.
There is a rat dead on a black bank,
where polyps of mushrooms bloom
like tiny skulls out of the darkness
and a moth shuts a delphinium's eye.
I do not feel you dreaming anymore,
but I know the moment sleep
touches down it taxies you here,
and I can hear your breathing
frosting the pane between us:
an image of white wings alighting
and anchoring itself to our thoughts
before it evaporates like our thoughts —
we still wear the moistures of the air,
water binds us to water but somewhere
out there something else is moving
across the surface of reflection.

Ex Ponto

A life raft drifts across the ocean
but never finds a harbour —
it is a phantom craft ringed by fire
and ice and ghosted where it goes
by an albatross and a white whale,
seals nose it into storms just to watch
the waves buffet and break it on the surf ...
Some say it is the orphaned midden
of a ship that once battled the high seas
and now must bear its lost cargo
of damned souls forever on the tides.
At dusk it is filled with naked infants
who huddle against the icy spray —
you can hear their wails at night at sea,
but at break of day they change to gulls
then fly away till darkness drops again.
Fishing boats have seen it and called in
mad maydays just before they too vanished.
And so onwards it floats, rudderless
into the wide and anchorless blue.

LESSNESS

Red sands shift along the ridge and the dunes eddy
and slide like avalanches down its slopes–
This is the pattern of the East, advance, retreat,
with the sun baking your brain inside your mind.
Across the slave distances the stones are worn rough
and you inhale their windblown dust. Isis blinks
and her sarcophagus sinks and in an instant
the desert floor is swept clear of everything but itself.
I wonder what you would make of all this, father.
Could I transport our love here and find an oasis to slake
your dying tongue, let it whisper and sigh as over the sea
I heard your cry in the emerald wind? I brought you
out here in my heart and now I find you everywhere,
in that Bedouin's eyes, in this goatherd's rheumy hands.
The time between us is not measured by sun or sand,
and though I cannot read their signs I do know this,
it will soon be time to climb the air to reach you over there:
the light I have you have already lost, and the night you had
will soon enough be mine, so let us go and meet then
between the crescent moon and the already absent sun.

The Broken

I am coming undone one seem at a time,
and the pretence of right is all wrong.
I scan the future for a flicker of before,
but know in this deepest wounded heart,
whose pulse is fast fading and whose tendons
grow weary of their endless toil,
that this darkness will never lift again.
Only you can stir these slow bones now
except your bones have paled into absence,
and I cannot wait until the eye dims water
or the lens clings to its film for tomorrow?
Who will say I was worth it at the end?
and who will stay the hand that conspired
against itself? There is a warmth I'm missing
and miss no matter what and all the tropes
I've made cannot raise even one degree.
What pools at time's feet is not pity's blood
or tears that cannot shed an idle thought —
but the gathering of falling to pieces, and now
I know it's past putting them back together.

Epilogue

I am dying through my father's dying,
the way his white thoughts go grey
as ash on the screen of his going –
they picture spectral motions there
that come into focus then evanesce,
and now the credits are running,
rhyming absence with time
and our name with its patronymic.
What can be done once the story's done?
Nothing remains where we stood, only rocks
beating back the sea, and then the sea,
but our love still swims there, father,
goes deep as the bottom, is weighed upon,
sinks and rises and then comes ashore
on choiring lips of foam.
This requiem is as old as the earth itself,
as it rinses the flesh with ancient tears,
daubs the bones, white-washes the marrow
and delivers ciphers of sand and dust
the very next surf will wipe away.

ABOUT THE AUTHOR John A. Griffin was born in Tipperary, Ireland. He attended St. Louis University and Washington University (USA), where he read for his PhD. He currently lives and works in Riyadh, Saudi Arabia. He sometimes blogs new work at odradek-poetry.blogspot.com.

ABOUT THE ILLUSTRATOR Martine Mooijenkind is a collage artist from Gouda, The Netherlands. "I can browse through books for hours to gather pretty images and after a while new worlds emerge, dream worlds. I start and the rest follows naturally. The worlds just happen." A creative game. Cut and paste. Glue, paper and scissors. In other words; the old fashioned way of Photoshop.

FEATURED COLLAGES

Cover	Lost
Pg. 2-3	Water on the moon
Pg. 12-13	Gentle
Pg. 24-25	Angst

ABOUT THE PUBLISHER The Esthetic Apostle was founded in 2018 out of Chicago, Illinois. The publisher promotes content expressing the beautiful and sublime through self-realization. This is their first title featuring a single poet. The Esthetic Apostle produces an online magazine monthly featuring poetry, prose, artwork, and photography, and a print issue quarterly.

For more information, visit www.EstheticApostle.com

www.ingramcontent.com/pod-product-compliance
Lightning Source LLC
Chambersburg PA
CBHW041811040426
42449CB00004B/152